# FunTime® Piano

## LEVEL 3A-3B

### 中国乐曲

## MUSIC FROM CHINA

*Arranged by Nancy and Randall Faber*

This book belongs to: _____

Topic Planning: Yishan Zhao
Production Coordinator: Jon Ophoff
Editor/Researcher: Patrick Bachmann
Translator/Editor: Lin Tian
Design and Illustration: Terpstra Design, Wagner Design
Engraving: Dovetree Productions, Inc.

ISBN 978-1-61677-727-2

# A NOTE TO TEACHERS

**FunTime Piano Music from China** is a colorful, pianistic collection of folk songs and original Chinese piano works for early intermediate students. The pieces were carefully selected for appealing dance-like rhythms, dramatic movement across the keyboard, sonorous use of the pedal, as well as faster tempi with crisp articulations.

The pieces explore fascinating elements of China including flowing canals, elephants, the famous peacock dance, the moon in the cultural history of China, and imitative mountain songs. In this collection:

- **Introductory notes** are given.

- **Performance tips** help with interpretation.

- **Illustrations/photos** are offered for musical inspiration.

- **Duet Improvisations** and a **Guided Student Composition** help students create their own "sounds of China."

**Helpful Hints:**

1. Hands-alone practice is often helpful to focus on fingering and melodic and rhythmic patterns. Pieces may also be broken down into sections for focused learning.

2. Difficult passages may be flagged for special practice. Consider colored pencils to mark these as "achievement passages."

3. In Chinese music, it is especially important to pay close attention to the articulation and dynamics. This will help the music to "dance" with exciting contrasts—for a performance full of vitality.

4. The student may go through several **FunTime Piano** books, which feature a variety of styles, before moving up to **BigTime Piano** (Level 4 and beyond).

Hi, I'm **LeLe** (pronounced Luh-Luh)* the musical panda from China. Look for me in the book for important music pointers!

FunTime Piano

* The Chinese character 乐 "Le" has two meanings, one is music and the other is happy!

# CONTENTS

## Introduction to *Northwest Rains* (pp. 6-7)

"Northwest Rains" originated as a nursery rhyme sung in the southern Fujian dialect. The northwest rain referred to thunderstorms that would disappear just as quickly as they came on summer afternoons.

Its fun lyrics talk about intense rains and warn farmers to leave the rice fields as they will soon be flooded with eels (snake-like fish).

Translated lyrics:

*The northwest rains fall straight down, and the egrets hurry on their way.*

*Crossing mountains and rivers, can't find the way and get tripped.*

*Can't believe the sun is going down.*

*To grandmother and grandfather earth: Please lead the way with your good heart.*

*The northwest rains fall straight down.*

**Teacher Duet: (Student plays HIGH on the keyboard)**

\* as often as desired

## THE SOUND OF NORTHWEST RAINS

"Northwest Rains" (**pp. 6-7**) is based on the **A natural minor scale**.
The A natural minor scale is related to the **C major scale**.

**1.** First, play the **C major scale**. Listen to the *major* sound.

### C Major Scale

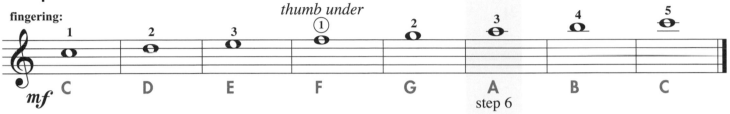

**2.** Now play the **A natural minor scale**. Listen to the *minor* sound.
   Notice it begins on **A** (scale step 6) and uses all the *same* letter names.

### A Natural Minor Scale

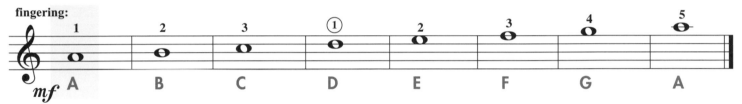

The **A natural minor** is the *relative minor* of **C major**.
They are "related" because they share all the *same* notes.

### Duet Improvisation Activity

• Your teacher will play the duet on **p. 4** based on "Northwest Rains."
  Listen to the **tempo** and **mood**.

• When you are ready, create your *own* sounds using the **A natural minor scale**.
  Play the notes *in any order*. Here are a few ideas to explore:

• End on any **A**. Consider using a **trill**
  from **A** to **B** to finish this piece.

6

**LeLe's Questions**

1. What is the main **interval** used in the Introduction and Coda? _____

2. What do you think could be happening in the rainstorm at **m.*  20**? **m. 21**?

西北雨直直落
**Northwest Rains**

Southern Fujian Children's Folk Rhyme

INTRODUCTION

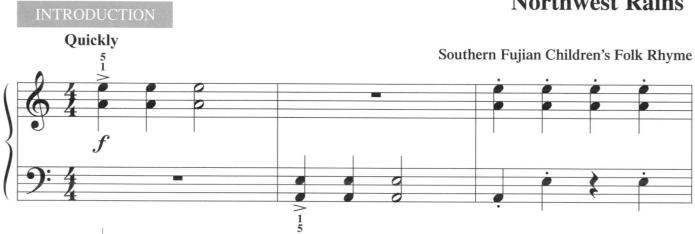

THEME

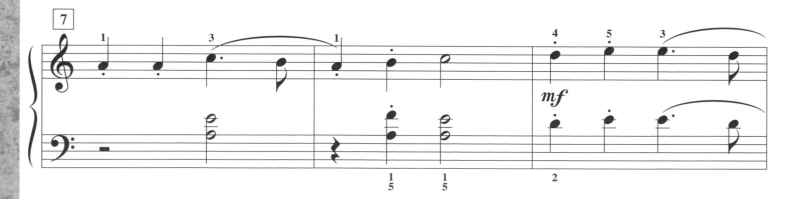

\* **m.** – abbreviation for measure

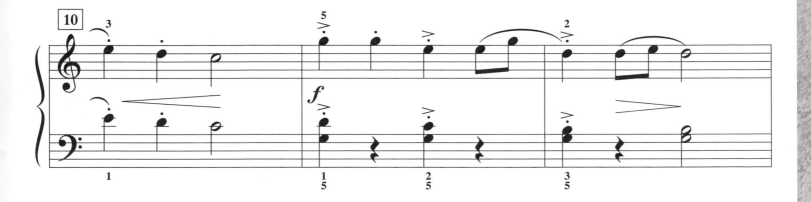

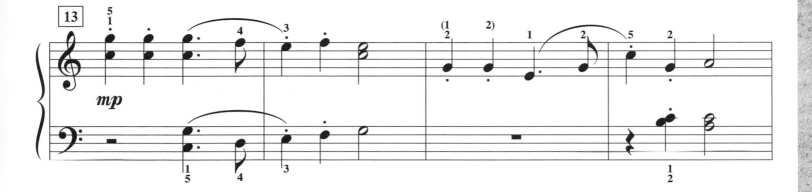

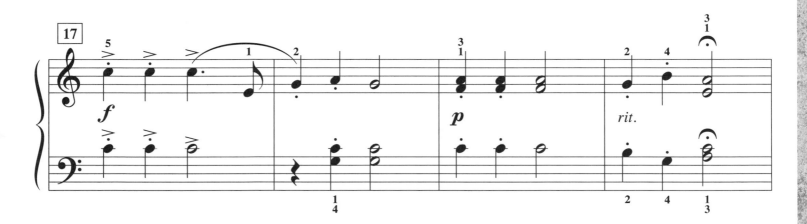

CODA

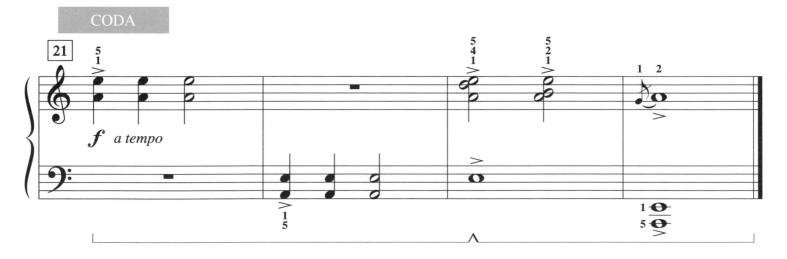

## Introduction to *The Flowing Canal* (pp. 9-11)

A canal is an artificial river connecting one place to another and allows boats and ships to travel inland. Did you know that China has the longest and oldest canal in the world? It is called **The Grand Canal**.

This canal is indeed grand being over 1,100 miles in length. Constructed around 2,500 years ago, this canal weaves through mountains, towns, cities, and farmland. In some periods of history, more than 8,000 boats would transport over 300,000 tons of grain.

## Performance Tips for *The Flowing Canal*

**1.** In this piece, the **R.H. 8th notes** moving back and forth suggest the sound of a gently flowing canal. This pattern flows throughout the entire piece.

Play the R.H. softly with a "quiet hand," staying *close to the keys*.

**2.** "Sing" or "voice" the **L.H. melody** as you play. Notice the interesting L.H. articulation—*staccatos within a slur*. "Portato" is the name given to this special articulation.

Gently "ring" these notes using a little more arm weight.

**3.** Let's imagine what these notes could be:

- raindrops falling into the canal?
- a gentle wind dropping seeds into the canal?
- a school of fish swimming underneath?

**LeLe's Questions**

1. Can you find *two* passages where the hands play
   a **G** **(add 6)** broken chord up the keys? *
   Beginning at: **m.** _____ and **m.** _____

2. How many beats does each *whole rest* receive
   in this piece? _____

水渠流呀流
# The Flowing Canal

Composed by Li Chongguang

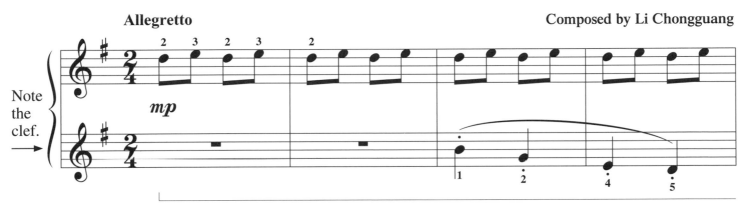

Pay close attention to the **pedal marks** to give an underwater, flowing sound.

\* **G** **(add 6)** = **G** chord (G-B-D) with an **added 6th** from the G major scale— **E.**

10

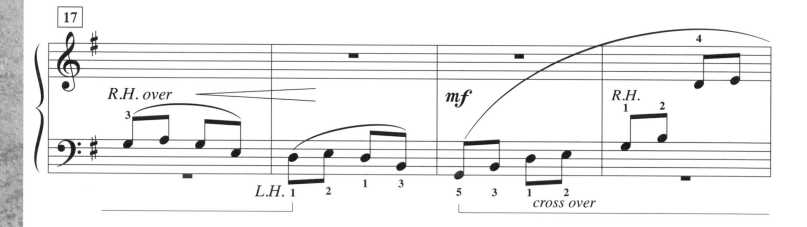

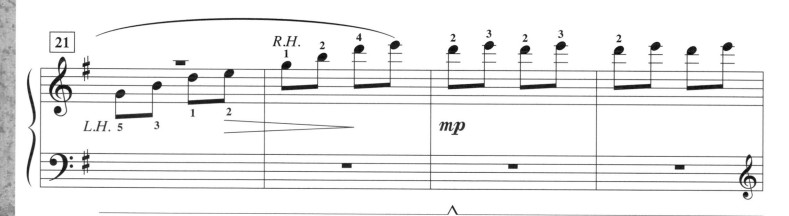

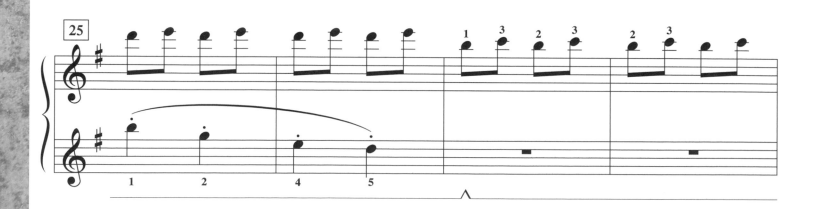

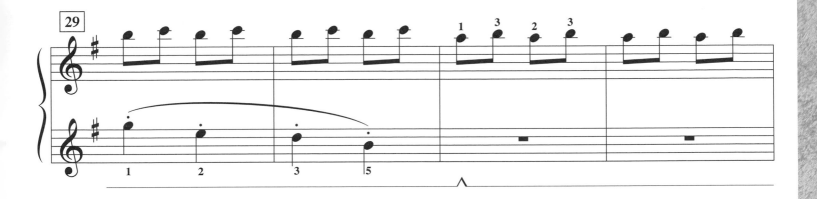

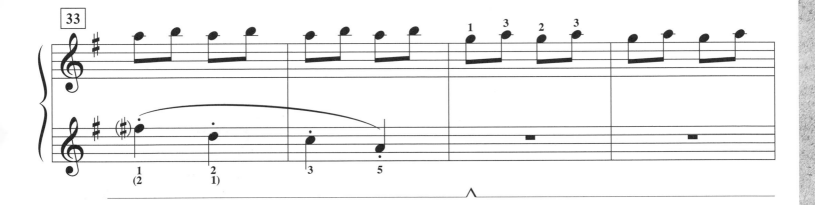

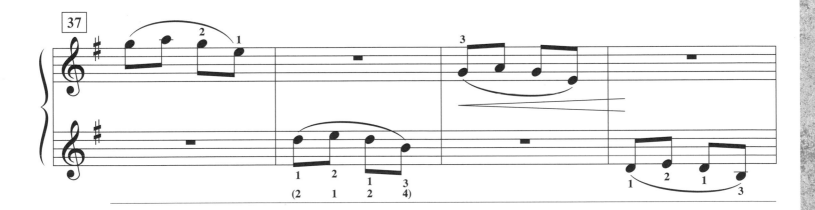

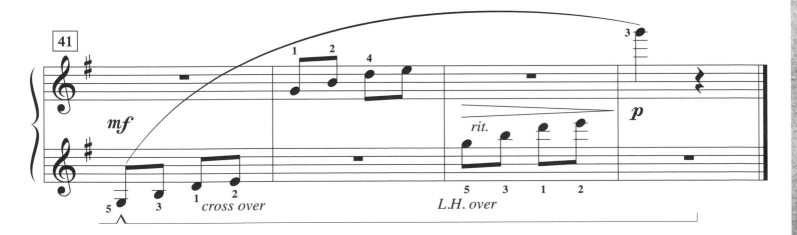

## Introduction to *Elephant* (pp. 14-15)

In Chinese culture, the elephant is a symbol of strength, hard-work, kindness, wisdom, and luck.

The Chinese pronunciation for elephant is da xiang (pronounced: da shih ahng). "Xiang" sounds very similar to the Chinese word for "lucky." On top of that, the cloth on the elephant's back represents good fortune and peace.

Asian elephants grow to about 6 and a half feet to almost 10 feet tall at the shoulder. Their weight can range from 4,500 to 11,000 pounds!

## Performance Tips for *Elephant*

**1.** In this piece, the rocking **5ths** split between the hands remind us of a slow, lumbering elephant. The musical gesture here is a **two-note slur**.

- Drop with **arm weight** into the first 5th with the *tenuto mark*.
- Use *less* weight on the next 5th, lifting gently for a "soft sigh."

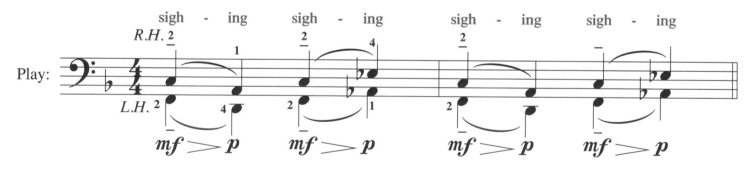

**2.** In several places, the **R.H.** melody *descends*—like the trunk of an elephant swinging down.

- Shape the melody with *cresc.* and *dim.* to add to the swaying effect.

## CREATING A JAZZY "ELEPHANT WALK"

**1.** This **F "blues" pentatonic scale** includes steps **1**, **2**, **3**, **5**, and **6**, plus the **flatted 3rd** (A♭). Practice it ascending and descending until it's easy.

**2.** Can you **memorize** this scale?

**F "Blues" Pentatonic Scale**

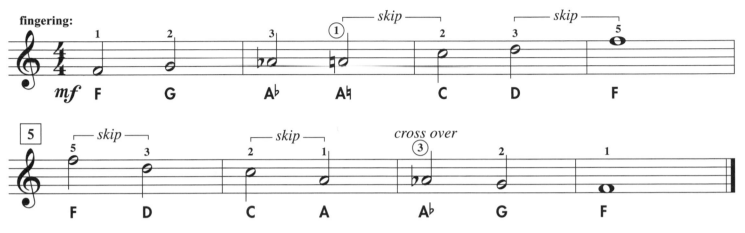

### Duet Improvisation Activity

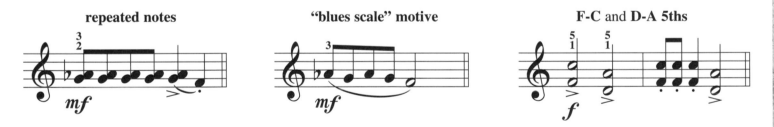

- Your teacher will play this duet based on "Elephant." **(pp. 14-15)** Listen to the **tempo** and **mood**.

- When you are ready, create your *own* melody using the **F "blues" pentatonic scale** shown above. Play the notes *in any order*. Here are a few ideas to explore:

**Teacher Duet: (Student plays HIGH on the keyboard)**

14

### LeLe's Questions

1. This piece ends **pp**. What could the elephant be doing? Use your imagination!

2. Spot two passages where the L.H. plays *ascending* **5ths**.
   Beginning at: **m.** _____ and **m.** _____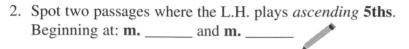

大象
**Elephant**

Composed by Li Yinghai

Andante (♩ = 64)

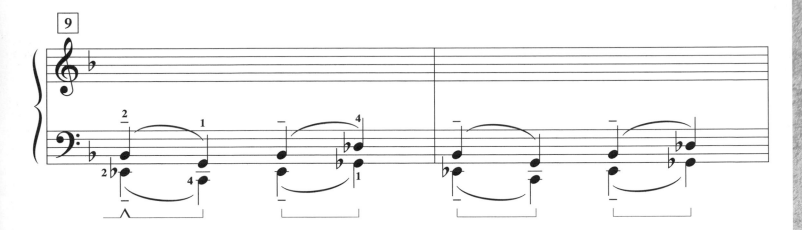

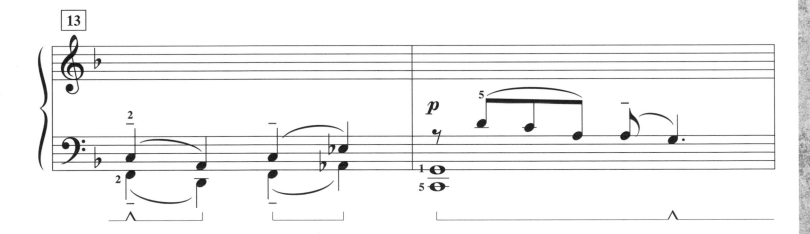

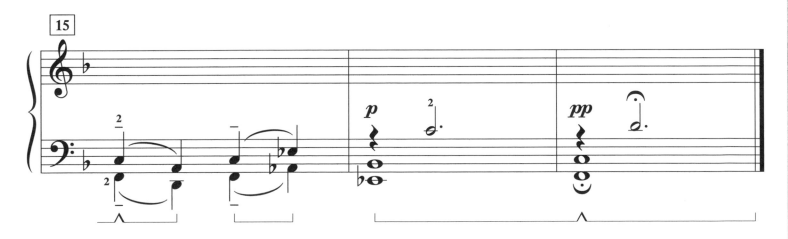

## Introduction to *Peacock Dance* (pp. 18-19)

The peacock dance is a traditional dance from the Dai people in southwest China—leaders in singing and dancing for almost 2,000 years! Folklore tells that 1,000 years ago, a Dai leader was walking by the river and saw a beautiful peacock dancing. He was drawn to imitate the graceful gestures of the bird. This eventually became the peacock dance and has been passed down for many generations. The dance usually has a specific order:

- The peacock flies from its nest and looks around.

- It wanders about looking for food.

- After eating, it bathes and plays by the river.

- It shakes off the water, grooms its feathers, and plays in the sun.

- It ends by fanning its beautiful wings and flies into the sky with happiness.

## Performance Tips for *Peacock Dance* (pp. 18-19)

**1.** The most important thing to remember is that this is very much a **dance**. The rhythm must be very *strict* with a proud, *strutting* quality.

- Look through the piece. How many times does the L.H. play this **dance pattern**? ♩ ♩ ♩ _____ ✐

**2.** This peacock dance is a **Theme and Variation**. Circle **3 things** that are *different* in the Variation than in the Theme.

   a. There is a key change.
   b. The L.H. moves an octave lower.
   c. Accidentals are added for color.
   d. A coda (ending) is added.
   e. The dynamics change.

# THE SOUND OF A PEACOCK DANCE

Like "Northwest Rains," this piece also uses the **A natural minor scale**.

1. Can you finish writing the **scale** and naming the notes?

2. Practice this **A minor scale** *ascending* and *descending* for fluency and speed.

## A Natural Minor Scale

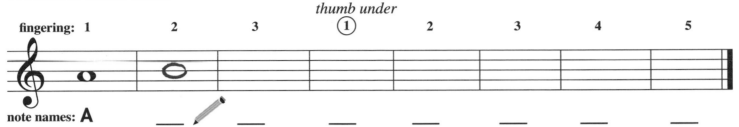

## Duet Improvisation Activity

• Your teacher will play a "proud duet" based on "Peacock Dance" (**p. 18**). Listen to the **tempo** and **mood**.

• When you are ready, create your *own* sounds using the **A natural minor scale**. Use short **repeated patterns** to create the character of a "peacock dance." Here are a few ideas to explore.

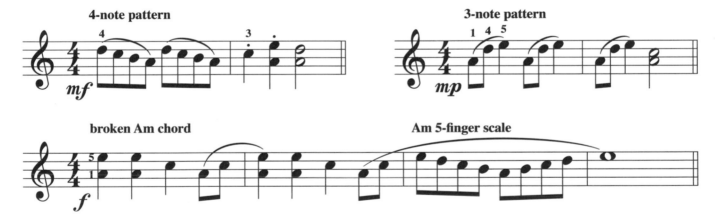

**Teacher Duet: (Student plays HIGH on the keyboard)**

18

**LeLe's Questions**

1. In **mm.*** **5-6**, are the hands playing in *parallel* or *contrary* motion? _____

2. What might be happening during the peacock dance at the *final* measure?

孔雀舞
### Peacock Dance

Arranged by Li Feilan

THEME

**Moderato**

DOWN _____ up      up

Notice how the pedal marks help accentuate the dance gesture.

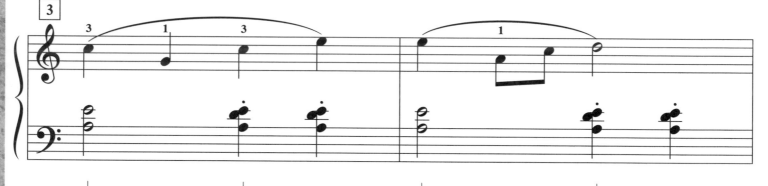

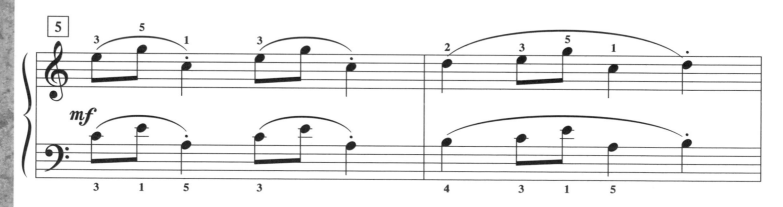

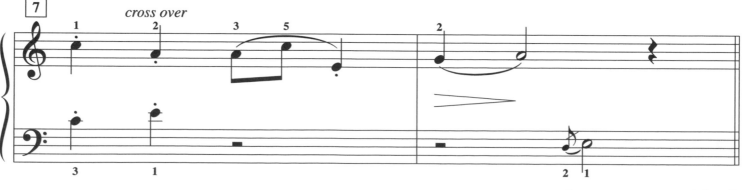

*cross over*

***** **mm.** – measures (plural)

VARIATION

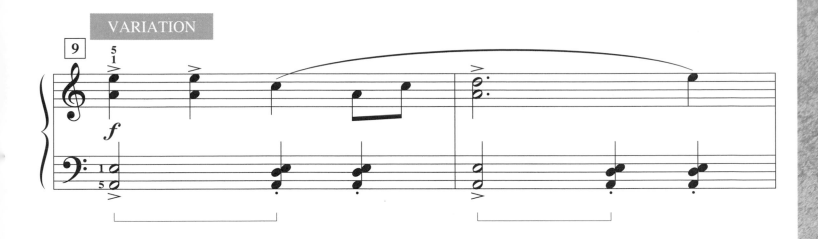

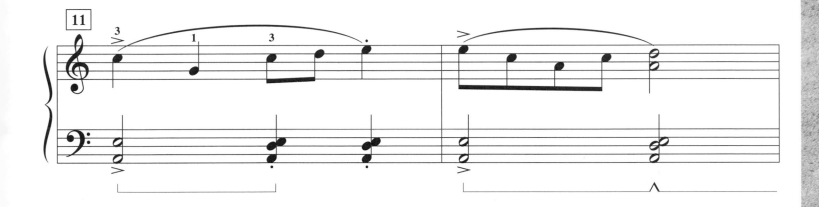

cross over

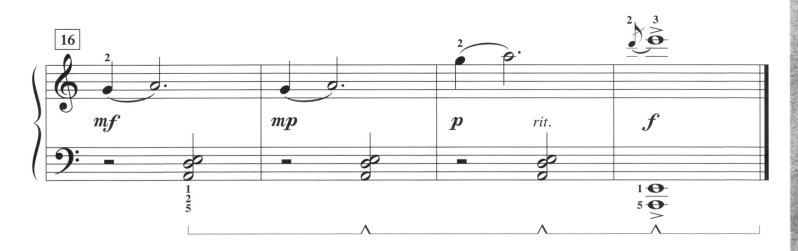

## Introduction to *Gazing at the Moon* (pp. 21-23)

In Chinese culture, the full moon represents peace, prosperity and, most importantly, togetherness. The Chinese Moon Festival or Mid-Autumn Festival is celebrated on the 15th day of the 8th month of the lunar calendar.

On this day, families will gather together and share a round, sweet pastry dessert called mooncakes. Often at night, it is a tradition to gaze up at the full moon. For those apart from their families on this day, gazing at the moon has a special meaning — that in spite of our physical distance, we all stare at the same moon.

HAPPY
*Mid Autumn*
FESTIVAL

## Performance Tips for *Gazing at the Moon*

**1.** The **4-measure introduction** sets the mood for this piece.
Notice the R.H. chords in **mm. 1-2** "fall," like moonlight shining down.

- Play these *mf* chords back and forth a few times, lifting gracefully.
This dynamic might remind us of the "bright lunar light."

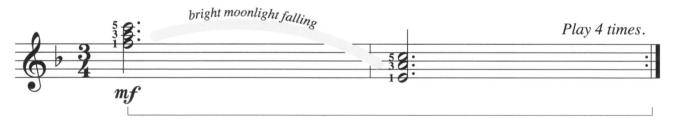

**2.** Notice the chords in **mm. 3-4** also fall. The **A-flat** creates an **F minor chord**.

- Play these *p* chords back and forth, lifting gracefully.
This dynamic might reflect a soft, mysterious glow.

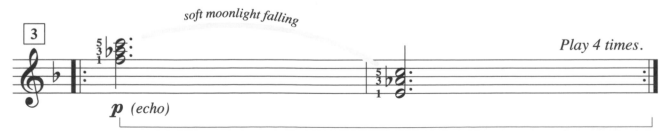

## Performance Tips, continued

**3.** The L.H. plays a flowing **8th-note accompaniment** that requires a "quiet," steady hand.

- Play the **L.H. alone** for the entire piece noting the *pattern changes*.
  **Hint:** Circled finger numbers will alert you.

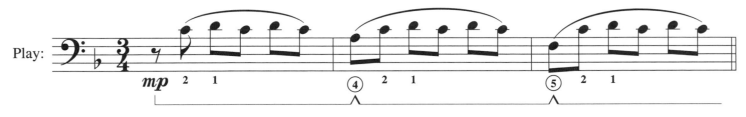

**4.** At **m. 5**, the **R.H. melody** features soaring, arching phrases.
   Imagine a full moon and play these notes with a full, round tone.

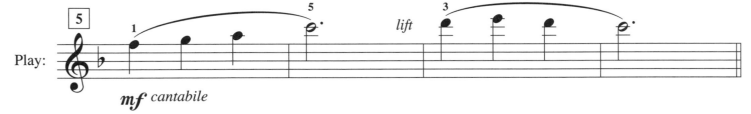

*Comodo* (comfortably fast) at **m. 1** and *cantabile*
(singing) at **m. 5** guide the tempo and mood.
Let the soaring lunar melody "shine brightly."

看月亮
**Gazing at the Moon**

**Composed by Li Feilan**

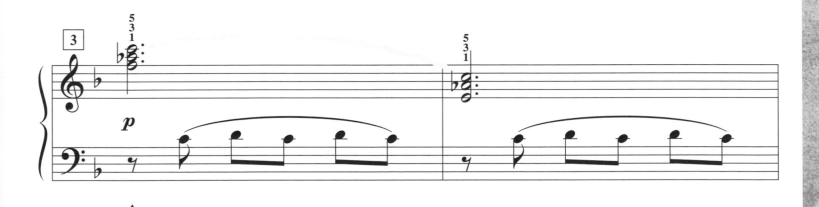

22

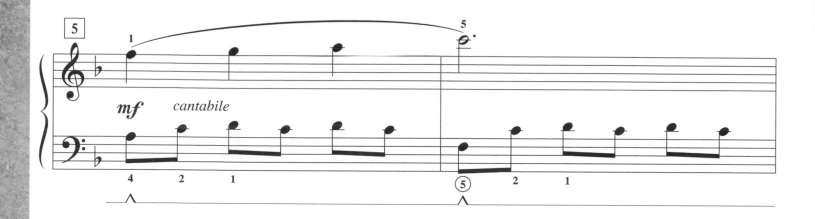

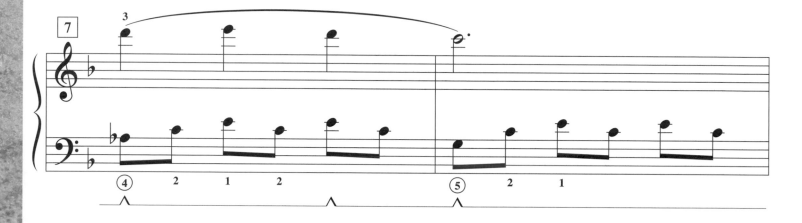

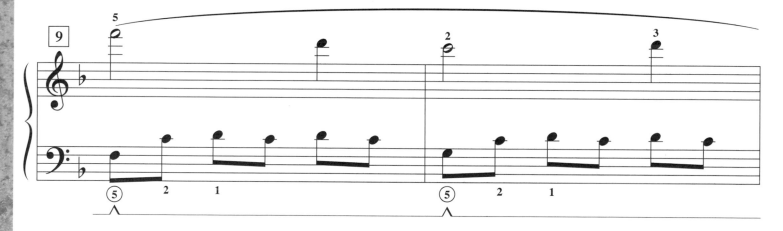

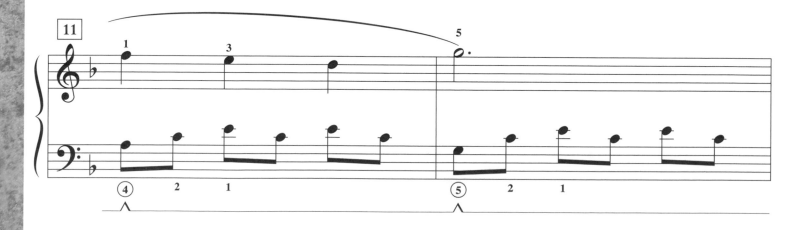

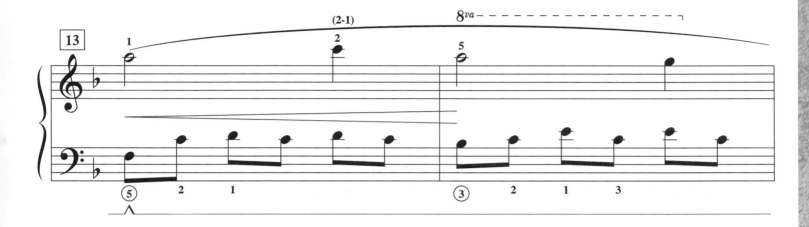

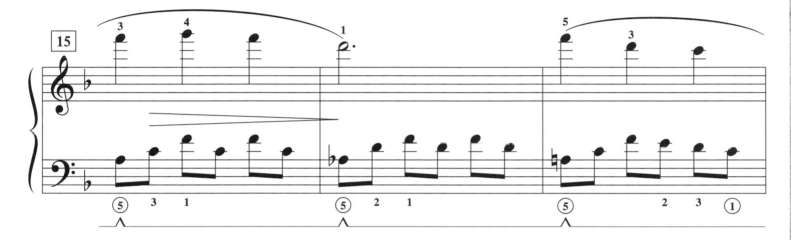

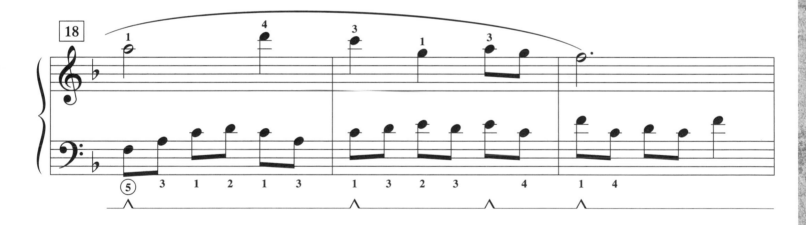

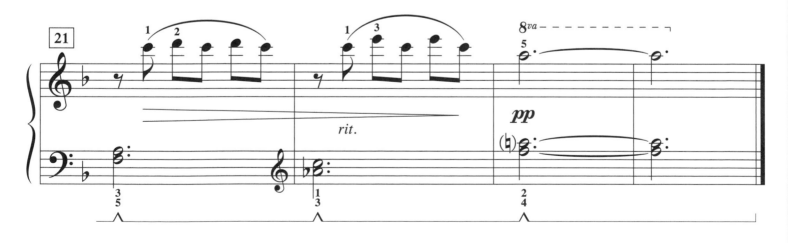

24

## Introduction to *Mountain Song* (pp. 25-27)

Mountain songs are most often heard in rural provinces. Common features of mountain songs are **call and response** melodies (similar to question and answer) and **imitation**. This is inspired by the echo that you would hear if you were to sing full voice on top of a mountain.

## Performance Tips for *Mountain Song*

**1.** In **m. 1**, notice the 3-note *ascending* motive.

Think of calling out someone's name.
Stress the opening note with the *tenuto* mark.

**2.** In **mm. 2-3**, the **R.H.** plays a long, descending cascade of notes.
It ends with the opening 3-note motive one octave lower.

*Imagine the sound being carried down the mountain!*

**3.** At **m. 3**, the **L.H.** enters.
Does it also cascade down and end with the opening motive?

**4.** At **m. 7**, the **L.H.** "calls out," starting on **D**.
Does the **R.H.** imitate in **m. 8**? Name the accidental used in this section (**mm. 7-10**). _____

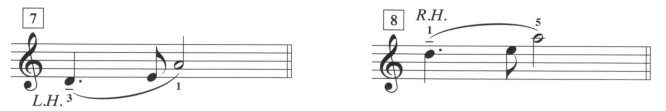

**5.** The overlapping theme continues. Imagine voices "echoing" around the mountain.

- Practice **hands alone** at first, noting the fingering and melodic patterns.

- Play **hands together** s-l-o-w-l-y. Add the pedal when you are ready.

山歌
**Mountain Song**

**Composed by Li Yinghai**

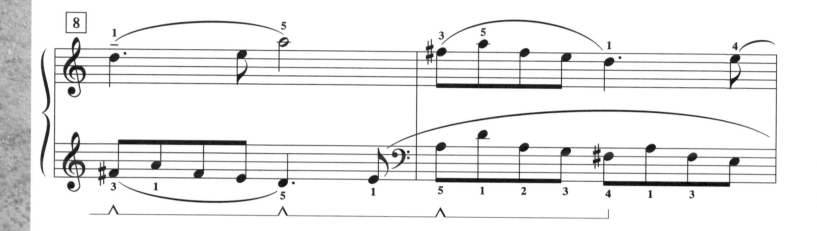

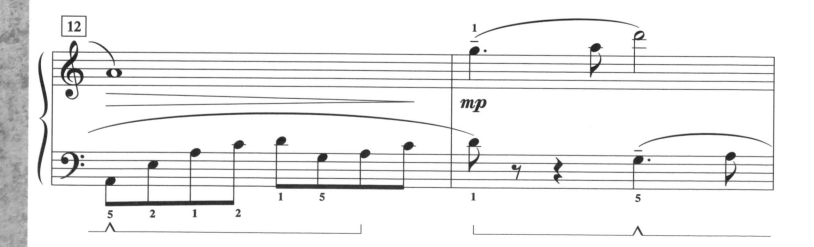

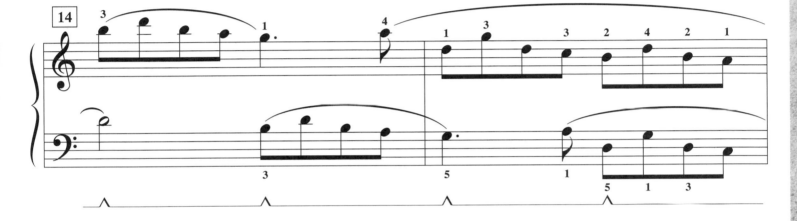

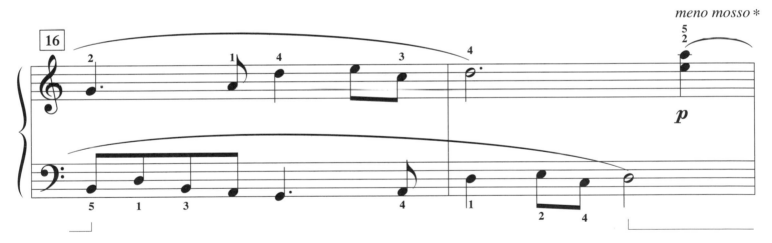

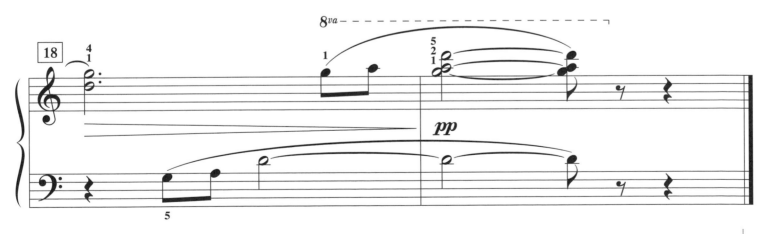

* less motion, slower

## The Composer Is You!

In this book, two pieces are based on the **A natural minor scale**:
"Northwest Rains" (pp. 6-7) and "Peacock Dance" (pp. 18-19).

Compose your own piece with these steps:

- Play the L.H. **ostinato** (repeating pattern).

- Create your *own* R.H. melody using the
  **A natural minor scale.** A sample rhythm
  is shown in **blue** starting at **m. 3**.

- The final R.H. note can end on **A**, the *tonic* ("home note").
  Or, explore a mystery note that "hangs in the air."
  The L.H. **A** pedaled in **m. 16** will create a
  "home note" sound.

**A natural minor scale**

_____
**Title**

_____
**Composer (your name)**

**Flowing gently**

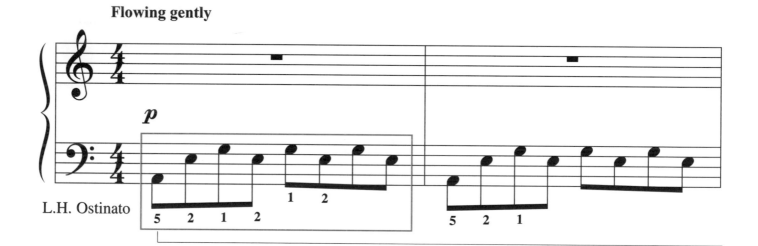

L.H. Ostinato

\* **Dal Segno al Coda**: Return to the 𝄋 "sign", and play to the **Coda** ⊕ mark.
Then jump to the **Coda** (ending).

# DICTIONARY PUZZLE

Use terms from the
**Music Dictionary (p. 32)**
to complete the puzzle.

## ACROSS

1. *pp*   Very soft.

3. _____   Singing melody.

5. _____   Medium speed.

6. _____   Rather fast tempo.

9.    Hold this note its full value.

10. _____   Less motion; slower.

12. **¢**   **2/2** time. 2 half note beats per measure.

13. └────┘ A sign to depress the pedal.

14.    Hold this note longer than usual.

16. *rit.*   Gradually slow down.

17.    Play this note louder.

18. ◁   Play gradually louder.

19. ▷   Play gradually softer.

20. _____   Return to the original speed.

22. *8va* ⌐ Play one octave higher than written.

**DOWN**

2.      Walking speed.

4.      A musical form which starts with a theme that is then altered or "varied" through any given number of variations.

7.      The main melody of a composition.

8.    *p*     Soft.

10.      Abbreviation for *mezzo-piano*.

11.  *ff*   Very loud.

14.  *f*   Loud.

15.      An ornamental note played quickly into the note that follows.

21.      The abbreviation for *mezzo-forte*.

# MUSIC DICTIONARY

| | | | | | |
|---|---|---|---|---|---|
| *pp* | *p* | *mp* | *mf* | *f* | *ff* |
| *pianissimo* | *piano* | *mezzo-piano* | *mezzo-forte* | *forte* | *fortissimo* |
| very soft | soft | medium soft | medium loud | loud | very loud |

**crescendo (cresc.)**
Play gradually louder.

**diminuendo (dim.)** or **decrescendo (decresc.)**
Play gradually softer.

| SIGN | TERM | DEFINITION |
|---|---|---|
| > | **accent** | Play this note louder. |
| | *allegretto* | Rather fast. |
| | *andante* | Walking speed. |
| | *andantino* | A little faster than *andante*. |
| | *a tempo* | Return to the original tempo (speed). |
| | *cantabile* | Singing melody. |
| ⊕ | *coda* | Ending section. |
| | *comodo* | A comfortably fast tempo. |
| ¢ | **cut time** | $\frac{2}{2}$ time. 2 half note beats per measure. A ♩ (instead of a ♪) gets the beat. |
| 𝄐 | *fermata* | Hold this note longer than usual. |
| ♪ | **grace note** | An ornamental note that is played quickly into the note that follows. |
| | *meno mosso* | Less motion; slower. |
| | *moderato* | Medium speed. |
| | **ostinato** | An accompaniment based on a repeating pattern. |
| $8^{va}$ – ┐ | *ottava* | Play one octave higher than written. When $8^{va}$ – ┘ is below the staff, play one octave lower. |
| ‿ᐱ‿ | **pedal change** | Lift the damper pedal as the note (or chord) is played. Depress the pedal immediately after. |
| └─┘ | **pedal mark** | Depress the damper pedal after the note or chord. |
| | **pentatonic scale** | A 5-note scale common in Chinese music. (Ex. C-D-E-G-A) |
| *rit.* | *ritardando (ritard.)* | Gradually slow down. |
| ̄⬝ | **tenuto** | Hold this note its full value. Hint: Press deeply into the key. |
| | **theme and variations** | A musical form which starts with a theme that is then altered or "varied" through any given number of variations. |
| | **theme** | The main melody of a composition. (Many works have more than one theme.) |